Embrace
Consciou:

CW00505114

Your Best Meditation Guide

Table of Contents

Foreword

One of the easiest ways to cultivate more happiness and peace in life, meditation helps to build intuition and self-esteem, make skillful, wise choices, hear your truth, better communication, and boost productivity and creativity. If you're reading my book, chances are you've decided to bring more consciousness into your life. Even a 15-minute meditation practice can significantly change your life.

If you're a beginner though, you might not know how to meditate to reap maximum benefits. I've been mediating for over 10 years and today my day isn't complete without meditation. In this book, you're going to find out how to use meditation practices on a daily basis and get rid of many health woes.

Meditation seems to be complicated at first since most of us have trouble taking control of the mind. Once you master it though, you'll significantly boost your mental and physical health, fight stress, increase your productivity, and maximize your ability to concentrate, and stay conscious about what's happening around you.

People who meditate on a daily basis experience less stress, anxiety, and worry, and tend to be more productive, positive, successful, healthy, and happy. Enjoy learning the basics of meditation and ways to incorporate it into your daily routine.

Section 1: What Is Meditation?

Chapter 1: Meditation Exists Beyond Your Mind

The state of thoughtless awareness and blissful consciousness, meditation provides a unique opportunity to transform your mind on an intricate spiritual level. It allows you to foster new, fulfilling, and positive ways of "being." Meditation isn't about doing or effort; it's just a state of spiritual awareness.

When it comes to meditation though, your mind is totally helpless because all it can do or achieve isn't connected to meditation. Your mind is not capable of penetrating meditation. Meditation begins where your mind ends.

Many people believe that meditation is all about sitting quietly with closed eyes in a lotus position and doing nothing. That's the major reason a lot of us believe meditation is boring and has no benefits.

When it comes to meditation, your mind can do nothing regardless of how hard you put it to it. Your mind can't meditate, so if you've ever tried to meditate and failed, it's because you didn't reach the point beyond your mind.

There are plenty of methods and techniques that help to maximize your meditational experience and discover your true nature. The techniques I'm going to share with you in the next section will teach you to connect with your mind, take control of it, and free yourself from it.

The emptying of the mind is necessary for a successful meditation session. I often hear people say, "I can't achieve the meditative state; I can't meditate." First of all, I want you to understand that meditation isn't your goal or achievement. It's your true nature that is already exists within you but is still unexplored.

Each of us has been carrying meditation since childhood. While some people manage to discover it once they grow up, others die without knowing their true Spirit nature. If you're reading my book, chances are you're striving to let your meditation thrive. You're looking for something more in life – more well-being, more energy, more peace of mind, more happiness, or more meaning.

As you patiently and consistently learn how to go beyond your mind, you'll gradually create an intensely powerful, peaceful, and happy life. Meditation will lead and guide you in truth and provide you with a new understanding of life.

I like to consider my meditation practice as a journey of sorts. As ridiculous as it sounds, I have my own destination – a destination where I feel joyful and happy. Meditation helps me reach that destination, offering numerous alternative routes.

Chapter 2: Meditation Benefits

Meditation boasts a wealth of health benefits besides fighting stress. When I first started meditating, I couldn't even think about how it would change my entire life. Meditation has made me happier, healthier, and a lot more successful. It has improved my social life, my self-control, and my productivity.

We live at an extremely chaotic, stressful time where our nervous system suffers most, triggering a host of diseases and conditions, including heart issues and cancers. Hundreds of studies have been conducted to prove the health benefits of a regular meditation practice and here are some of the best ones:

1. Strengthen the immune system

A research conducted at the Ohio State University that involved cancer patients found that relaxation aids in boosting the immunity in the patients. A strong immune system significantly speeds up the recovery process, preventing new health woes. The daily progressive muscular relaxation can even lower the risk factor of breast cancer.

I couldn't boast about good health until I started my meditation journey. I spent tons of money on medications that eventually didn't cure but hurt my body. The core reason of my poor health was a weak immunity due to my stressful life.

Meditation promotes relaxation that gives your body a greater resistance to viruses and tumors. No wonder doctors recommend people with cancer meditate on a daily basis.

2. Boost fertility

Multiple studies have indicated that women who are more relaxed and less stressed are more likely to conceive than those who have a stressful lifestyle. On the other hand, men with the high stress levels tend to have reduced sperm count and motility. Meditation provides relaxation that increases male fertility.

3. Reach emotional balance

When your emotions are balanced, you're free of the neurotic behavior as a result of the existence of a traumatized and tortured ego. It's tricky to fix such a neurosis and harmful emotional state, but meditation can do the trick.

Once you're free of emotionally soaked memories, you'll be able to achieve emotional balance and bring happiness and positivity in your life. Emotionally balanced people always recommend meditation, stating that it's a great way to live mindfully.

4. Regulate blood pressure

Researchers from Harvard Medical School revealed that a regular meditation practice helps to lower the high blood pressure similar to blood pressure-reducing medications. When you meditate, your body becomes less responsive to stress hormones, which typically cause blood pressure spikes.

5. Alleviate the symptoms of irritable bowel syndrome

Practicing meditation at least twice a day can help you ease the symptoms of irritable bowel syndrome, such as constipation, diarrhea, and bloating.

6. Fight inflammation

Chronic inflammation leads to various health issues, which is why it's critical to keep it at bay. Stress is the leading cause of chronic inflammation that's linked to asthma, arthritis, heart disease, and skin conditions, including psoriasis.

7. Calm your mind

My life has never been "peaceful." Maybe, it's because of my overthinking habit or because the modern world is too demanding. I had trouble getting sound sleep and waking up with a calm mind. Meditation was my best solution. It helps to calm the mind, tame morning anxiety, and promote a better sleep. The meditative mind switches off stress, takes better decisions, and breeds positive thoughts.

Chapter 3: How Meditation Works

With a growing number of meditation forms, ranging mostly in complexity from general recommendations to strict, regulated practices, it's sometimes hard to understand how meditation works. However, once you start your meditation journey, you will soon realize the beauty of meditative mind.

If you practice meditation on a daily basis, it will help to develop unconscious, habitual micro-behaviors, which will produce enormous positive effects on your psychological and physical functioning. Even a quick 15-minute meditation practice twice a day can bring amazingly beneficial results.

It's all about parasympathetic response. A lot of theories indicate that meditation is a complex form of relaxation that involves a concept of the parasympathetic nervous system. The part of the involuntary nervous system, the parasympathetic nervous system helps to relax the sphincter muscles, boost glandular and intestinal activity, and slow the heart rate.

The psychological stress is linked to the sympathetic component activation of the autonomic nervous system that can cause the 'fight or flight response.' Any form of meditation decreases the sympathetic activation by lowering the production of catecholamines and some other stress hormones like cortisol, and enhancing the parasympathetic activity that improves the blood flow to the viscera away from the periphery and slows the heart rate.

Other researchers suggest that meditation provides the special neurophysiological effects. A study done by the Meditation Research Program found that the limbic system is more likely to be involved in Sahaja Yoga Meditation because the drastic effects involving the mood swings have been consistently watched.

Chapter 4: Meditation in Action

One of the most important steps to successfully integrating meditative mind into your awareness is by using the things and actions happing throughout the day as part of your meditation practice. Each one of us perceives the world in our own way. The way you perceive each experience in your everyday life can bring you deeper into the meditative space.

On the other hand, this form of meditation isn't for newbies as it requires experience and firm grounding. With meditation in action, you should keep functioning effectively and even stay alert while you meditate. Once you master the basics of meditation, mastering meditation in action should be priority as well.

Meditation in action will eventually help you start living a conscious life, which will create a meditative space within you. The meditative space stands between every response you make and thing you notice, providing a spacious, quiet, and peaceful view of the entire universe.

I'd never thought about the importance of meditation in action until I got stuck in the big city rut that made me feel down. I could barely meditate and my life lost its meaning. As I kept practicing a regular meditation, I expanded my meditative space. Today I find that even a tiny action like walking in the park can be a great meditative experience.

When walking in the park, I stay quiet and peaceful inside – either through watching my breath or mantra. This allows me to experience my consciousness and watch the things around me in the new light.

Every time my consciousness awakes, it triggers some desire system, like a desire for success, happiness, or love. The desires are different so when I stay in the meditative space, I avoid getting lost in them.

Meditation in action uses the techniques that let you notice the moment-to-moment experiences. Each experience is here to serve you. Each experience is here to awaken you. Meditation in action is closely related to karma yoga. These two open the path of awakening through daily activities.

Be it sleeping, eating, earning a living, or marrying, you see each action as an act provided to God. Each action becomes a meditation in relation to God. When you finally learn how to meditate, you'll be able to master the capacity to meditate from the very moment of waking up to the moment of falling asleep. You'll learn how to stay at ease and alert in this super busy world. The moment to moment daily living will become an absolutely freeing and blissful experience.

Section 2: How to Incorporate Meditation into Your Life

Chapter 5: How to Prepare for Meditation

I believe meditation is less about quantity but more about quality. If you have never meditated before, you may need to prepare yourself and your mind for the first session. The benefits to meditation mentioned in Chapter 2 happen thanks to what it is you are doing in the practice.

Meditation is not magic, pointless navel-gazing, or blissing out. You're taking an advantage of the way your mind functions in the natural world, focusing on the adaptability of your brain. This triggers a self-directed neuroplasticity, which is an awesome feature of the meditation practice. Meditation can intentionally change the physical structure and the functioning of your brain.

However, it's critical to prepare yourself – and particularly your brain – for your first and further meditation sessions. You might be wondering what it is that you are going to do during meditation. To be short, you're going to do several basic things:

- You will be bringing your full attention to the present moment. This part of meditation will help you begin to break your tendency to be unaware of what's going on around you. Plus, it will prevent you from spending time in the past that you can't change anyhow or the future that you can't predict and depend on.
- You will observe and realize what's happening in the present moment. It will weaken your habit of wrongly identifying yourself as the body, thoughts, feelings, or things happening around you.
- You will set aside all the judgments about what you see and experience. This will help you detach from the narratives that usually guide your actions. You will eventually realize that you should guide your actions.

Then, you can widen the focus of your attention to encompass a great variety of phenomenon or limit it to one single object, while still staying in the present moment. No matter which technique you use, you are mastering the skills that help you reflect and respond faster during the troubles and challenges of everyday life, instead of expressing aversions, thoughts, or negative emotions.

As soon as you understand the idea of what you're going to do and experience in meditation, it's time to prepare yourself for it. Here are a few things you should do:

1. Prepare a quiet space

People who have been practiced meditation for years can meditate anywhere – literally. However, if you're just starting, it's best if you prepare a special, quiet space for your meditation session. Simple things such as sitting in a special place, turning off your cell phone, or lighting a candle can enhance your meditation practice. Just like you put on your running shoes before your workout, you need to gear up for meditation too; because as soon as you put on your running shoes, the body starts preparing itself for a run. The similar principle can be applied to your meditation sessions.

Have a special, small space in your room or house for your meditation sessions so that every time you're in this place, your body knows it's time to prepare for meditation. You can also play certain relaxing music for meditation to give your body a sign. But we'll talk about the pros and cons of playing music during meditation later in this book.

2. Wear comfortable clothing

Wear the pieces of clothing that you're sure are comfortable and will not distract you. If your clothes make your body stiff during meditation, you won't be able to concentrate. Consider wearing loose clothing that will let you feel more relaxed and at ease. Don't wear any shoes.

3. Do a few preliminary stretches

Stretching will help you wind down any tension in your muscles and body. Start with stretching out your neck muscles and head. Perform a few leg stretches to prevent the pressure on them while you'll be sitting cross-legged during the meditation session.

4. Set an intention

Before meditation, be sure to set an intention. It's a simple way to get the full value and meaning of your meditation session. Setting an intention creates a direction for you and helps you find an answer to your biggest questions. If you consciously establish an intention before meditation, you'll be able to align with the true purpose of your practice.

The most important question to ask yourself is, "Why do I meditate?" There are plenty of reasons, but you should know your own one. Whether you want to meditate to figure out the peace that exceeds understanding, or experience God consciousness, or find an excuse to catch a nap, your intention will help you get the most benefits out of your meditation sessions.

5. Get ready for distractions

Unless you live in a forest, tons of distractions can ruin your meditation. You might end up worrying about your job, going over your to-do list, or simply thinking about the latest news you watched today. Or, your kids, friends, or whoever lives with you can interrupt. That's why make sure you get ready for any distractions.

Write down a short list of the biggest distractions that could spoil your meditation and think about the ways to avoid them. If you fail to free your awareness from these distractions, your meditation session will more likely to be unsuccessful.

6. Learn how to focus

People who start meditating, always have difficulty to focus and meditate. If you need a way to start your meditation, try asking yourself some meaningful questions, like "Who am I?", "What's my purpose of life?", "What am I grateful for?" etc.

Chapter 6: How to Meditate

If you're just interested in starting a meditation journey in order to see what it's all about or reap the benefits of meditation listed above, there's a great tendency for different types of meditation to consider. Each type of meditation has the same basic techniques and principles with some variation. However, the instructions I'm going to share with you below are usually compatible with many types of meditation. Once you acquire a foundation of a basic meditation session, you can try out other types.

Here are some forms of meditation to choose from:

- **Mindfulness meditation**: This one encourages you to focus on wandering thoughts as they're attacking your mind. Your intention isn't about getting involved with your thoughts and banishing them. Your intention is to stay aware of every mental note appearing in your mind.

  The mindfulness meditation allows you to see the ways your feelings and thoughts move in certain patterns. As you keep practicing mindfulness meditation, you'll become more conscious of your tendency to judge an experience as bad or good, unpleasant or pleasant, in a matter of a few seconds. With practice, you'll develop an inner balance that will help you overcome your overthinking habit.

- **Concentration meditation**: This form involves a complete concentration on a single intention/subject/thought. Concentration meditation usually entails the breath, watching a candle flame, repeating a mantra or just single word, counting beads on a mala, or listening to a repetitive gong.

  Concentration meditation is tricky and challenging and a beginner has difficulty focusing the mind. Thus, it's recommended to meditate for only a couple minutes and gradually increase the time.

  Concentration meditation helps to refocus your awareness on a certain intention/subject/ thought every time your mind gets over-brimmed with thoughts. Instead of pursuing some random thoughts, concentration meditation makes you let them go. This type of meditation helps to improve concentration and tame anxiety.

There are many other types and techniques of meditation. For instance, Buddhist monks meditate on a daily basis to fully focus on the cultivation of compassion. It can be something like imagining some negative events and reconstructing them in a positive light by changing them through a form of compassion. Moreover, there are moving meditation techniques, including walking meditation, qigong, and tai chi.

Again, the instructions provided below will help you create an initial foundation of the knowledge and skills, which you will use in many other meditation practices, no matter how complicated they are.

You may want to try various forms and techniques in order to shift your meditation practice to meet the events happening in your life. You might want to practice one technique today and another one tomorrow.

So, how do you meditate? Follow the instructions below:

Step 1. Think about how many minutes you can spend meditating. Beginners tend to start with a 5-minute meditation while pros can meditate from 20 minutes to 2 hours. When deciding on the time, try to make sure it's at the same time daily.

Step 2. Do a few stretches to release any tightness or tension before you start.

Step 3. Sit in a comfortable position. When meditating, it's critical that you feel comfortable, so choosing the perfect position should be your goal. Generally, meditation is practiced in a sitting position. Just sit on a cushion on the floor or ground in either a half-lotus position or complete lotus position.

If you lack flexibility in your lower back, hips, and legs, you may experience discomfort. Even though it's recommended to sit with a straight, tall, and balanced posture during the meditation session, you can meditate lying in your bed.

If you don't like the idea of meditation on the floor or ground, invest in a meditation chair or bench. Comfort is the key here.

Step 4. Once you're in a comfortable position, concentrate on the rest of your back. Begin from the bottom of it and think about every vertebra in the spine. Imagine balancing one topping another to maintain the entire weight of your head, neck, and torso.

This step is about relaxing your torso and learning to ease any area of the body where tension hits. It you still feel discomfort, try to rebalance your torso to find the right position.

Step 5: Close your eyes. Since you're not a pro who can meditate with their eyes opened, close your eyes to avoid any visual distractions and get into a meditative mood.

Step 6: Breathe naturally. Choose a place above the navel and concentrate on that area with your mind. Stay aware and conscious of the increasing and falling of your stomach as you breathe in and out. Avoid changing your normal breathing patterns. Simply breathe naturally.

Step 7: Concentrate on mental images that appear in your mind. If nothing appears, try visualization. For instance, imagine a buoy peacefully floating in the sea, which is bobbing up and down with your each inhalation and exhalation. Or, you can imagine a beautiful lotus flower on your belly that unfurls its petals with each inhalation and exhalation.

Meditate this way for 2 to 5 minutes. If your mind starts wandering, don't worry. You can start your session again to regain your focus. Clear your mind and concentrate on one thing or object. Multithinking isn't for meditation.

If you fail to meditate in a complete silence, give mantra meditation a whirl. This is a form of meditation that involves telling and repeating a mantra – be it a phrase, word, or sound – over and over again until you clear your mind, tame your thoughts, and dive into a deep, meditative state.

When it comes to mantras, the popular yet simple word "Om" is a good way to start with. The word symbolizes the omnipresent consciousness and helps to banish any negative thoughts. You can also say other words, such as peace, one, calm, silence, and tranquil.

As soon as you enter a deeper meditative level of consciousness and awareness, you may want to stop repeating your mantra.

Chapter 7: Meditation Alternatives

Although meditation alternatives have fewer health benefits than a meditation itself, they're still some great options. Many meditation leaders recommend meditation alternatives, which allow you to meditate without meditation. Here are some of the most popular alternatives:

1. Belly laugh

It's the top alternative that actually boasts some awesome health benefits. A smile promotes your well-being while a good laugh lifts your spirit and ward off mental health issues like anxiety and depression. A regular belly laugh helps to gain an emotional balance and prevent mood swings.

2. Walking meditation

Often referred to as kinhin, this form of alternative meditation helps you stay aware of every tiniest thing happening around you. Whenever you feel tired, anxious, or depressed, take a long stroll in the park, concentrating on the motions of your body and your breathing. Let your body relax and enjoy the beauty of the world. Be sure to switch off your smartphone.

3. Dance

Dancing meditation is a rather new alternative yet it's simple and effective. Plus, this meditative activity is a powerful workout. You don't have to know how to dance professionally or take some classes. Just dance at home when you're alone or have your family members to dance with you.

4. Cleaning

When approached in the right way, your house cleaning can turn into a real meditation session. Whether it's doing laundry or dishes, vacuuming your room, washing a car or a bicycle, or mowing the lawn, cleaning helps to combat depressive thoughts, induce ideas, and give your body a time to connect to the inner self.

When cleaning, keep your mind empty, and concentrate on the chore you're doing at the moment. Your brain will then react in a similar way it would to meditation.

5. Mindful standing

Often called standing meditation, this form of meditation promotes a peaceful sense of internal stability and aids in reducing a lower back pain. Start slow, though. Try standing for in a straight posture 3 to 5 minutes first. You'll be astonished at what a 3-minute mindful standing will do to your overall well-being. Keep your mind clear and focus on your breathing.

6. A fixed-gazing meditation

Also called Trataka, this meditation alternative is a bit weird as it's about staring at a fixed or certain thing or object while sitting, standing, or lying. A fixed-gazing meditation helps to relieve headaches, boost the eye health, lower stress, and improve memory and concentration.

Whether outdoors or indoors, take a few minutes to choose an object and gaze on it. It can be a stone, flower, animal, tree, moon, stars, or any other object you like. No matter how long you gaze on your object, do it in a silence without any distractions.

7. Swimming

Swimming is an excellent meditation alternative, not to mention that it's a full-body workout. Swimming on a regular basis helps to build endurance and banish stress and anxiety. If you have no place for swimming or can't swim, consider taking a relaxing bath for about 20 minutes with no distractions.

8. Coloring books

Nowadays, coloring books for adults are a perfect alternative to meditation. Coloring a picture requires presence, patience, and good concentration. This helps to reduce the everyday tension and stay calm in a difficult situation.

9. Music

I don't mean your favorite songs here. I mean listening to the sounds of nature, special meditation music, or soothing and calming musical instruments, like piano, violin, harp, flute, or cello. Choose your favorite sound and listen to it when you are stressed or depressed, or before sleep. Ensure your family won't disturb you at this moment.

Chapter 8: Mindful Eating as a Part of Meditation

Mindful eating has been shown to help people cope with food cravings with a bigger intention and awareness. It's a practice that let you tune in to the needs of your body and be thoughtful about what you put in your body. Your health highly depends on how you nourish yourself.

By completely appreciating the textures and flavors of the foods you eat and being in the present moment while having your meal, you open yourself up to a more meaningful level of enjoyment. Mindful eating as a part of meditation will help you make healthier meal choices.

Here's how you can learn to eat mindfully:

1. Slow down

Your body needs time to catch up to the brain to let it know it's enough for food. Eating slowly gets your body and mind to communicate about what you need for nutrition. With a busy schedule, it seems impossible to eat slowly. But, your body takes nearly 20 minutes to send its satiation signal to the brain. That's the major cause of overeating. We eat fast, without listening to our body's signals.

2. Eat at a set time and place

Modern people have used to eating on the go and packaged foods. However, if you want to make your food consumption a part of meditation, it's time to break those bad eating habits. First, create a healthy eating environment. Sit down at a table, put your food on a plate, and use utensils to eat it.

Try to schedule your day so that you could eat at a certain time and preferably alone. This will help you munch on your meals mindfully. If you make your meal, cook mindfully as well.

3. Eat nutritionally healthy foods

Do you consume foods that are nutritionally healthy or emotionally comforting? We love it when food reduces stress or anxiety, but this food is more likely to be unhealthy. Think about where your food comes from and which nutrients it contains. Remember, eating healthy foods mindfully can cure even the most difficult diseases, including heart disease and cancer.

Afterward

One of the most challenging things about meditation is never starting. You can start anytime and anywhere, but the problem is continuing to practice meditation on a regular basis. Not every newbie manages to make meditation a part of their daily routine. Even if you've tried meditation and really like the feelings and benefits it provides, the activities, distractions and problems of your everyday life can ruin your most sincere intention to meditate.

It's okay to miss your meditation session every now and then, but if you're truly serious about reaping the benefits of meditation and start living a more peaceful life, try your best to incorporate any form of meditation into your life and maintain it. You don't have to be a pro. My guide is sure to help you fall in love with meditation and develop your own forms of it even if you're a newbie.

Stay patient and exercise your mind to experience the beauty of a mindful, happy living. Now, it's time to start your journey...

Printed in Great Britain
by Amazon